English Conversations
For Children

Copyright © 2016 by Ralph Duncans Jr
All rights reserved.

English Conversations For Children

Ralph Duncans Jr.

ISBN: 978-0-9961766-4-4

Library of Congress Control Number: 2017907526

This is an English language workbook

My English Publishing
4287 Humboldt St
Detroit, MI, USA 48208

TABLE OF CONTENTS

From The Author...i
Let's Play Together..2
Let's Go Shopping..4
Please Come With Me..6
I Want To Sit..8
Nothing Special..10
Cookies...12
In The Morning..14
Lets Be Friends..16
Going Out...18
A Good Lunch..20
Sleepy...22
Mommy's Day..24
I Want To Play...26
A Day Outside...28
Earthquake...30
Have A Fun Day..32
The Weather..34
I Am Sleepy...36
Reading..38
Yesterday...40
Suddenly..42
On The Train...44
Your Room..46
Drawing...48
Presents...50
 Let's Meet Later..52
I Peeked..54
Homework..56
An Apple...58
In The Front Yard...60

FROM THE AUTHOR

I use these conversations are for children from two year old and above who are just starting to read. These are children's conversations. I use these this book in my classes I teach in Japan. My students really enjoy reading these conversations. I enjoy using this book in class. I hope you and your students or children will also.

Learning to read is very fun.

I want to thank Darius R. Brookins. Basically, he suggested to me to make the front cover look more colorful and attracting. After some thought and watching illustration tutoring videos and about four hours later of designing and thinking, the cover you see is my finished project.

my1english1@gmail.com

LET'S PLAY TOGETHER

A. Where are you going?

B. I am going home.

A. What will you do?

B I will play a game.

A. I want to play a game too.

B. Let's play together.

A. Thank you.

B. You are welcome.

35 words

DEFINITIONS

1. play -

2. together -

3. where -

4. home -

5. what -

6. do -

7. game -

8. want to -

9. too -

10. thank you

11. you are welcome

Let's Go Shopping

A. What are you doing?

B. I am reading a book.

A. Do you want to go shopping?

B. Yes, I want to go shopping.

A. What do you want to buy?

B. I want to buy ice cream.

A. Ok. Let's go.

B. Ok. Here I come.

43 words

DEFINITIONS

1. what -

2. read -

3. book -

4. you -

5. want to -

6. shop -

7. ice cream -

8. let's -

9. here -

10. come -

PLEASE COME WITH ME

A. How are you?

B. I am fine. Thank you. And you?

A. I want to go to the bookstore.

B. What time are you going?

A. I am going at 1 o'clock.

B. I want to go with you.

A. Ok. Please, come with me.

B. Ok. Thank you.

46 words

DEFINITIONS

1. please -

2. come -

3. with -

4. me -

5. bookstore -

6. time -

7. o'clock -

8. want to -

9. go -

10. ok -

I WANT TO SIT

A. What do you want to do today?

B. I want to go to the playground.

A. What will you do?

B. I want to sit on the swings.

A. Are you going alone?

B. Yes. Do you want to come with me?

A. Yes. Thank you.

B. Great! You are welcome!

48 words

DEFINITIONS

1. sit -

2. you -

3. today -

4. want to -

5. playground -

6. swing -

7. alone -

8. great -

9. thank you -

10. you are welcome -

NOTHING SPECIAL

A. I want to walk.

B. Where are you going?

A. I am going to the mall.

B. Are you going to shop?

A. No. I will not shop.

B. May I go with you?

A. Yes, please!

B. Oh, thank you!

36 words

DEFINITIONS

1. nothing -

2. special -

3. want to -

4. walk -

5. where -

6. mall -

7. go -

8. may -

9. yes -

10. thank you -

11. you are welcome -

COOKIES

A. I will go to the library.

B. What will you do at the library?

A. I want to read a cookbook.

B. What will you cook?

A. I will bake cookies.

B. I want to eat cookies.

A. Help me bake.

B. Ok. I am happy.

40 words

DEFINITIONS

1. cookies -

2. library -

3. at -

4. want to -

5. read -

6. cookbook -

7. cook -

8. bake -

9. cookies -

10. eat -

11. help -

IN THE MORNING

A. Good morning.

B. Good morning. How are you?

A. I am sleepy.

B. Go wash your face.

A. What are you cooking?

B. I am cooking your breakfast.

A. What do you want to drink?

B. I want milk.

35 words

DEFINITIONS

1. good -

2. morning -

3. good morning -

4. sleepy -

5. wash -

6. your -

7. face -

8. breakfast -

9. want to -

10. drink -

11. milk -

LET'S BE FRIENDS

A. How are you?

B. I am fine. Thank you. And you?

A. I am fine too.

B. What is your name?

A. My name is Tommy.

B. Where do you live?

A. I live in Wakayama City.

B. Let's be friends!

37 words

DEFINITIONS

1. friends -

2. your -

3. my -

4. name -

5. where -

6. live -

7. city -

8. let's -

GOING OUT

A. What will you do today?

B. I will go to the movies.

A. Who are you going with?

B. I will go alone.

A. Which movie are you going to see?

B. I am going to see something.

A. I want to go with you.

B. Ok. Thank you.

44 words

GOING OUT: DEFINITIONS AND QUESTIONS

1. going -

2. out -

3. to -

4. movie -

5. who -

6. with -

7. alone -

8. which -

9. see -

10. something -

11. want to go -

A GOOD LUNCH

A. What did you eat for lunch?

B. I ate a hamburger and a salad.

A. What did you drink?

B. I drank grape juice.

A. Where did you eat?

B. I ate at home.

A. How was it?

B. It was delicious!

DEFINITIONS

1. good -

2. lunch -

3. what -

4. eat -

5. ate -

6. hamburger -

7. salad -

8. did -

9. drink -

10. grape -

11. juice -

12. where -

13. home -

14. how -

15. delicious -

SLEEPY

A. I want to sleep.

B. Are you tired?

A. Yes, I am tired.

B. Do you want to eat dinner?

A. No. I am not hungry.

B. Ok. Good night.

A. Read a book to me please.

B. Ok.

33 words

DEFINITIONS

1. sleepy -

2. tired -

3. want to -

4. eat -

5. dinner -

6. hungry -

7. read -

8. me -

9. please -

1. Who is sleepy?

2. Who is B?

3. Is A hungry?

4. Can you read?

12 words

MOMMY'S DAY

A. Put your shoes on?

B. Where are we going?

A. We are going to the beach.

B. Can I swim in the ocean?

A. No. I want to eat and shop only.

B. I want to swim.

A. You can swim tomorrow.

B. Ok.

39 words

MOMMY'S DAY: DEFINITIONS AND QUESTIONS

1. mommy -

2. day -

3. put -

4. your -

5. shoe -

6. on -

7. where -

8. going -

9. to -

10. beach -

11. can -

12. swim -

13. ocean -

14. shop -

15. only -

16. want to swim -

17. tomorrow -

1. Where are they going?

2. What does A want to do?

3. What does B want to do?

4. What will B do tomorrow?

20 words

I WANT TO PLAY

A. Where is the cat?

B. The cat is in the kitchen.

A. I will take the cat outside.

B. What will you do?

A. I will play with the cat.

B. Do you want something to drink?

A. No. I am ok.

B. Have fun!

41 words

I WANT TO PLAY: DEFINITIONS AND QUESTIONS

1. where -

2. cat -

3. kitchen -

4. take -

5. outside -

6. do -

7. with -

8. something -

9. have -

10. fun -

1. Where is A?

2. Where is the cat?

3. Where will A play with the cat?

14 words

A DAY OUTSIDE

A. How are you?

B. I am good.

A. Where are you going?

B. I am going home.

A. Do you want to go to the park?

B. What will you do at the park?

A. I will sit next to the lake.

B. Really! I will go too!

44 words

A DAY OUTSIDE: DEFINITIONS AND QUESTIONS

1. how -

2. good -

3. where -

4. going -

5. home -

6. park -

7. what -

8. at -

9. sit -

10. next to -

11. lake -

12. really -

13. go -

14. too -

1. Where are A and B now?

2. How is B?

3. Where is B going?

4. What will A do at the park?

20 words

EARTHQUAKE

A. Did you feel the earthquake yesterday?

B. Yes! I was scared.

A. What did you do?

B. I got under the table.

A. I ran outside.

B. Going outside is dangerous.

A. I know, but staying inside is too scary.

B. Yes, that is true.

39 words

EARTHQUAKE: DEFINITIONS AND QUESTIONS

1. feel -

2. earthquake -

3. yesterday –

4. scared -

5. got -

6. under -

7. table -

8. ran -

9. outside -

10. going -

11. dangerous -

12. know -

13. but -

14. staying -

15. inside -

16. too -

17. scary -

18. that -

19. true -

1. Do you like earthquakes?

2. What happens during an earthquake?

3. How many earthquakes does Japan have in a year?

18 words

READING

A. What are you doing?

B. I am reading a book.

A. What is the name of the book?

B. The name of the book is **Toy**.

A. Is it interesting?

B. Yes! It is interesting.

A. Can I read this book?

B. Yes. It is interesting too!

41 words

READING: DEFINITIONS AND QUESTIONS

1. reading -   2. ~ ing -

3. doing -   4. book -

4. toy -   5. Interesting -

6. can -   7. this -

8. too -

1. What is B doing?

2. What is the name of the book?

3. What does A want to do?

4. How is the book?

21 words

YESTERDAY

A. Yesterday, I went to the library.

B. What did you do at the library?

A. I read a book.

B. Yesterday, I went to the park.

A. Why did you go to the park?

B. I wanted to sit outside.

A. Next time, I want to go with you.

B. Ok. Next time, I go I will call you.

53 words

YESTERDAY: DEFINITIONS AND QUESTIONS

1. yesterday -   2. library -

3. read -   4. went -

5. go -   6. wanted -

7. sit -   8. outside -

9. next -   10. time -

11. next time -   12. call -

1. Who went to the library yesterday?

2. Why did B go to the park yesterday?

3. What do you do at the park?

4. Yesterday, what did A do?

21 words

SUDDENLY

A. It is hot outside.

B. I want to go somewhere.

A. Where do you want to go?

B. I don't know.

A. Do you want to go to an amusement park?

B. Yes! Which one do you want to go to?

A. I want to go to the one in Nagashima.

B. I want to go too!

51 words

SUDDENLY: DEFINITIONS AND QUESTIONS

1. suddenly -

2. it -

3. hot -

4. outside -

5. want to go -

6. somewhere -

7. where -

8. know -

9. amusement -

10. amusement park -

11. which -

12. one -

1. How is the weather?

2. Which amusement park does A want to go to?

3. What is at an amusement park?

4. Why does A want to go to the amusement park in Nagashima?

5. Why does B want to go too?

38 words

ON THE TRAIN

A. The train is crowded today.

B. The train is crowded everyday.

A. I want a car.

B. You are only seven years old.

A. It is ok.

B. You cannot drive.

A. Yes, I can.

B. No, you cannot drive.

A. I drive in my dreams.

B. Ok. Then go to sleep please.

49 words

ON THE TRAIN: DEFINITIONS AND QUESTIONS

1. on -

2. train -

3. crowded -

4. today -

5. everyday -

6. want -

7. car -

8. only -

9. year -

10. years -

11. old -

12. seven years old -

13. cannot -

14. drive -

15. can -

16. dream -

17. sleep -

18. then -

19. please -

1. How old is A?

2. What does A want?

3. Where are they?

4. What can you do in your dreams?

18 words

YOUR ROOM

A. Where is the book?

B. It is on my bed.

A. Can you go get it?

B. You can go in my room.

A. I do not want to go in your room.

B. Why not?

A. Because, your room is dirty.

B. My room is clean.

A. Really? I do not believe it.

B. Believe it. My room is clean.

56 words

YOUR ROOM: DEFINITIONS AND QUESTIONS

1. where -

2. it -

3. on -

4. bed -

5. can -

6. get -

7. in -

8. not -

9. do not (don't) -

10. because -

11. dirty -

12. clean -

13. really -

14. believe -

15. it -

1. Where is the book?

2. Whose book is it?

3. Why does A not want to go in B's room.

4. How is B's room?

5. Is your room clean?

21 words

DRAWING

A. Do you want to draw?

B. Yes. I want to draw.

A. What do you want to draw?

B. I want to draw an apple.

A. Ok. Let's draw an apple.

B. Do you have paper?

A. Yes. I have crayons too. What color do you want?

B. I want green.

A. I want blue.

B. Wow!

51 words

DRAWING: DEFINITIONS AND QUESTIONS

1. drawing -   2. let's -

3. have -   4. paper -

5. crayons -   6. too -

7. want -

1. What does A want to do?

2. What color crayon does B want?

3. What colors are apples?

4. Have you seen a blue apple?

15. have ~ seen -

25 words

PRESENTS

A. When is your birthday?

B. My birthday is December the 25th.

A Really! Your birthday is on Christmas?

B. Yes. My birthday is on Christmas.

A. Do you get many presents?

B. No. I do not get many presents.

A. I want more presents for Christmas.

B. I want more presents for my birthday.

47 words

PRESENTS: DEFINITIONS AND QUESTIONS

1. present -

2. when -

3. birthday -

4. my -

5. December -

6. 25th (twenty-fifth) -

7. really -

8. Christmas -

9. get -

10. many -

1. When is your birthday?

2. Whose birthday is on Christmas?

3. What does B want for B's birthday?

4. What do you want for your birthday?

23 words

LET'S MEET LATER

A. I am going to the park.

B. I want to go to the furniture store.

A. Please, come with me.

B. I want to buy a table.

A. Let's meet later, when you finish shopping.

B. Ok. I will meet you at 5 o'clock.

A. Thank you. I am very happy.

B. It is ok. Let's go skating.

54 words

LET'S MEET LATER: DEFINITIONS AND QUESTIONS

1. let's -					2. later -

3. furniture -					4. store -

5. come -					6. with -

7. buy -					8. table -

9. finish -					10. shopping -

11. at -					12. o'clock

13. very -					14. skating -

1. What time will A and B meet?

2. What will B buy?

3. What will they do later?

4. Why does A want to go to the park with B?

27 words

I PEEKED

A. Do you know what you are getting for Christmas?

B. Yes. I know.

A. What are you getting for Christmas?

B. I am getting a bike, a television and a DVD player.

A. Wow! That is great!

B. What are you getting?

A. I don't know. Wait a minute! How do you know what you are getting for Christmas?

B. I peeked.

A. That is not good to do.

B. I always peek.

66 words

I PEEKED: DEFINITIONS AND QUESTIONS

1. peek -   2. know -

3. get -   4. television -

5. DVD player -   6. great -

7. wait -   8. minute -

9. wait a minute -   10. how -

11. for -   12. that -

13. not -   14. good -

15. do -   16. always -

1. When is Christmas?

2. What is B getting for Christmas?

3. What is A getting for Christmas?

4. Do you have a bike?

20 words

HOMEWORK

A. What time is it?

B. It is 5 o'clock.

A. I am going home.

B. Why are you going home?

A. I have to do my homework.

B. I have to do my homework too.

A. What kind of homework do you have?

B. I have math.

A. Math is hard.

B. Math is easy.

49 words

HOMEWORK: DEFINITIONS AND QUESTIONS

1. homework -

2. time -

3. it -

4. going -

5. home -

6. why -

7. have -

8. do -

9. too -

10. kind of -

11. math -

12. hard -

13. easy -

1. What time is it?

2. What do they have to do?

3. Do you like math?

4. What kind of homework do you have to do?

5. Is your homework hard or easy?

25 words

AN APPLE

A. I am hungry.

B. What do you want to eat?

A. I want to eat an apple.

B Ok. Here you are.

A. Thank you.

B. You are welcome.

A. This is delicious.

B. I eat one apple everyday.

36 words

APPLE: DEFINITIONS AND QUESTIONS

1. hungry-

2. eat-

3. want-

4. delicious-

5. everyday-

1. What does B eat everyday?

2. How is A?

3. What is delicious?

4. What kind of fruits do you like?

18 words

IN THE FRONT YARD

A. It is sunny today.

B. It is nice outside.

A. What are you going to do?

B. I have no plans.

A. Do you want to go to the movies?

B. No. I want to sit outside on the grass.

A. Let's have a picnic!

B. In the front yard?

A. Yes. Why not?

B. Yea! Why not?

1. front -
2. yard -
3. sunny -
4. today -
5. nice -
6. outside -
7. plans -
8. movie -
9. grass -
10. have -
11. picnic -
12. why -

49 words

IN THE FRONT YARD: QUESTIONS

1. How is the weather?

2. What does A want to do?

3. What does B want to do?

4. Where will they have a picnic?

5. Do you like picnics?

6. What is nice outside?

7. What do you do when the weather is nice?

8. What is your favorite kind of weather?

9. Where are they?

10. How old do you think they are?

61 words

www.ingramcontent.com/pod-product-compliance
Lightning Source LLC
Chambersburg PA
CBHW080811010526
44113CB00013B/2363